Empowering Bystanders to End Bullying in Schools

Christine R. Cohen, PhD, LSSP

AAPC
PUBLISHING

6448 Vista Dr.
Shawnee, KS 66218
www.aapcpublishing.net

6448 Vista Dr.
Shawnee, KS 66218
www.aapcpublishing.net

Publisher's Cataloging-in-Publication

Names:	Cohen, Christine R., author.
Title:	Stand by me : empowering bystanders to end bullying in schools / Christine R. Cohen.
Description:	Shawnee, KS : AAPC Publishing, [2018]
Identifiers:	ISBN: 9781942197379; LCCN: 2018933849
Subjects:	LCSH: Bullying in schools--Prevention--Handbooks, manuals, etc. | Bystander effect--Study and teaching--Handbooks, manuals, etc. | Helping behavior--Study and teaching--Handbooks, manuals, etc. | Assertiveness (Psychology)--Study and teaching--Handbooks, manuals, etc. | Power (Social sciences)--Study and teaching--Handbooks, manuals, etc. | Failure (Psychology)--Study and teaching--Handbooks, manuals, etc. | Problem solving--Study and teaching--Handbooks, manuals, etc. | Teachers--Handbooks, manuals, etc.
Classification:	LCC: BF637.B85 C64 2018 | DDC: 302.34/3--dc23

Artwork: Shutterstock.com and Vecteezy.com
This book is designed in Frutiger.
Printed in the United States of America.

TABLE OF CONTENTS

This book is dedicated to all the members
of my large, unruly, and perfect family,
who have always stood by me.

1.

BACKGROUND AND HISTORY

What do children say when they are asked, "Have you ever been bullied or bullied others?"

"I have been bullied. Sometimes I will cry at home." [Why have you been bullied?] "Just for being me."

"People have been bullying me since third grade. They always call me a chicken head and everything. If I tell the teacher, they say they haven't."

"A kid kicked me and punched me. He kept doin' it. It was first grade. I walked away and told the teacher."

"I have not bullied others, but have been bullied … on the playground and during lunch. In third grade, I was swinging. A big girl walked up and pulled my swing back, hard. It threw me on the ground. She laughed and got on the swing."

"[I've been bullied] my whole life. They were making fun of me. At school, I just go tell the teacher. Sometimes it helps and sometimes she won't listen."

"I've been bullied a lot because of my weight. My fists start to clench and my face gets red. I want to punch them, but I don't. I don't usually tell anyone unless it gets out of hand."

"I've been bullied by a friend in second grade. A friend wanted me to play a trick on a teacher. I really didn't want to, but I did, and it made me sick to my stomach."

"I haven't bullied anybody else, but I have been bullied. I was bullied for a long time … in daycare and first grade. I wasn't like others. I was misplaced. I didn't have any of the things that others had, and I wasn't athletic like I am now. I came home crying every day. In kindergarten I was actually picked on by one of my teachers. She was never satisfied with anything I did. I strive to be the best, but I can't please everybody."

(Sample of responses taken from STAND BY ME interviews)

The Problem of Bullying

Bullying has been everywhere in the news. In 2007, I had the idea of teaching students simply to stand with a victim. The idea of being a presence on behalf of someone else led to ideas about how that might be encouraged. A lot of those ideas were predicated on knowledge of human behavior and how it works, gained from my training in psychology. I approached my local school district about piloting the STAND BY ME program. The name was always meant to be a description of its core tenet: that simply being with another person has great value. It began at the middle school campus, grades seven and eight, because the principal was willing to take a chance on it. In 2009, at the district's request, we extended it to the fifth and sixth grades as well. The data collected through 2014 are presented here. This is what is important:

- Kids don't live in a world of legislative definitions. They all know what bullying is and they're passionate about it. They are the ones who see it.
- When we ask them, their language is more intense than that of adults. They may assign words like "horrible," "cruel," and "violent" to inci-

dents that seem relatively minor to us. A lot of these experiences don't rise to the level of severity required for an administrative response.

They have their own definitions:
1. "Anything that will hurt someone else. [It] doesn't have to be pushing or hitting … it can be words."
2. "Like violence, but with words or hurting people's feelings."
3. "It looks like something that really should not be done, 'cause it can affect others in ways we don't understand …. They may look okay on the outside, but hold it in. And, you don't know, they may let it out in ways that hurt others."

STAND BY ME Addresses the Problem of Bullying

STAND BY ME is a way to respond to what we, as adults, cannot see.

STAND BY ME EMPOWERS BYSTANDERS TO ACT. It is a simple program that produces powerful results. It shows that children want to help - want to do the right thing - if they are given the tools to do it. At the same time, it is supported by sound behavior principles that provide a rationale for the way it is done.

> STAND BY ME is a simple but profound change in the way we address bullying. As one fifth-grade member said, it is the "courage in words; the following of actions; to teach; to be, not what people think of you, but to be a leader, not a follower."

The following data is from a sample of 43 student interviews conducted with applicants wanting to join the program:
- 32 of the 43 students (74%) reported having been bullied. The nationwide percent for 4th through 8th grades is 90%.
- Nine of the 43 students, or 20%, reported having bullied others.
- Six, or almost 14%, of the students reported being both victims and perpetrators.

Interviewees were also asked, "What keeps students from speaking out or doing something when they see bullying happen?" The numbers below reflect the number of students giving the specified reason. Some gave more than one.

Reasons	#
Afraid of being targeted	12
Want to see fighting	4
Don't want to get in trouble	4
Scared	4
Being hurt	3
Being hated by others	3
Are friends with the bullies and afraid of losing them as friends	3
Don't know what to do	2
Don't want to be involved/indifferent	2
Don't know who's doing it	1
Want to be cool	1
Don't want to be made fun of	1
Don't want to get into a fight	1
Embarrassed	1
Have anger issues and can't handle it	1
Want to handle it themselves	1
Don't like the person being bullied	1

Before STAND BY ME, if someone wanted to track the frequency of bullying at a campus or in a district, they would have to rely on discipline records, which generally include only actionable events that meet policy standards (i.e., legislative definitions) in districts. STAND BY ME addresses the smaller interactions that can loom large for children but are often dismissed by adults as tattling. It encompasses the children's definitions of bullying. In addition, it is a story not only of intervention but also of prevention.

Development of STAND BY ME

As a psychologist, a licensed specialist in school psychology, and an autism coordinator for a public school district, I have spent 24 years working with children and families, the last 17 of them specifically with children who have some form of autism spectrum disorder (ASD). Because these children do not "blend in" easily, they are often the targets of bullying, and because they have difficulty regulating their emotional responses, they inadvertently "reward" the bully by blowing up and saying inappropriate things that get them into trouble. Some examples I have heard include, "I'll kill you!," "I'll blow up this school and everyone in it!," "I know how to destroy you!," and "I'm going to pick up this chair and smash you!" For these children, these statements are a way of expressing their intense anger. For school staff, they are incendiary statements that often result in severe disciplinary penalties for the already victimized student.

The idea for this program came from a desire to create a support system for children on the spectrum, especially those in the upper-elementary and middle-school years when peers are the givers of status and adults are comparatively less interesting. As the STAND BY ME program has evolved, it has been beneficial for all children who are bullied – whether or not they have ASD.

STAND BY ME is a peer-led program that requires very little training. It creates an immediate support system for students targeted by bullies, and it gives teachers and administrators important information about where and when bullying occurs. That is particularly important because, in the same circumstances, students tend to describe bullying in more intense terms than adults do. They see and experience its impact in a way adults do not.

> If we want to stop the impact of bullying on students, we must respect their definitions. It is those definitions that matter.

Incidents that do not rise to a level that requires disciplinary action by administrators still take their toll on children. Until now, administrators have not had effective ways to deal with them. In schools, simplicity is everything; training has to be continuous, but no one has time to take on additional responsibilities.

In addition, teachers in grades where state testing looms large are less willing or able to spend energy creating and maintaining social programming. This program was developed on a school campus and takes into account the needs, time constraints, and structure of school.

STAND BY ME began in 2007 on a middle school campus. In subsequent years since, it has successfully moved into the upper-elementary grades. The program continues to be student-led with the students themselves doing most of the problem solving – their solutions have always been much better than mine.

2.

PROGRAM RESULTS: DATA

Ongoing data collection is one of the things that makes STAND BY ME stand out. Public schools are required to implement data-based programming. STAND BY ME members give schools numbers for decision making. In considering how to evaluate the success of bullying programs, the emphasis has been on whether or not student bystanders can and will act, given training in a set of simple skills. The data kept by schools typically do not include incidents that fail to meet the legal definition of bullying, and the assumption here is that much of the distress caused by bullying never gains a disciplinary foothold. The intent is to engage students and provide faculty support for a wide range of incidents.

STAND BY ME members are trained for two kinds of interventions: "Stepping Forward," which means they help a victim directly, and "Standing Back," which means that there is physical aggression involved, so they alert an adult.

The robust, yet simple data collection system created for STAND BY ME is readily understood and used by students. In this program, students are taught to record interventions, locations, and types. They mark where they saw an incident and whether they stepped forward to help a victim or stood back and alerted an adult. The program is designed for students to take the program and run with it.

Data from 4-Year Pilot Program

STAND BY ME was implemented on three campuses in one school district, although we struggled at grades seven and eight due to inconsistent faculty sponsorship. In order to get the best idea of the number of students generating the data, the average number of participating members was reported, rather than the number of members on the program rosters. Participation meant the number of students attending meetings, and not every student reported data at every meeting. The numbers are conservative, because one campus sponsor counted only the students reporting data. (The data summary sheet that resulted in this lack of clarity has been revised.)

Although Year 4 participation appears to drop (see graph below), it is artificially low. Because the sponsor was having problems with members not wearing their ID logos to meetings, she allowed only those students with ID logos to report data, so the number for that campus does not even reflect meeting attendance. Again, this number, as with all the data, has been reported very conservatively. For instance, in Year 3, the average number of students participating in meetings at grades seven and eight was reported, but because the data was not separated into types of interventions, not added to the total.

Data from this program over a 4-year period is reported here. The graph shows the numbers of interventions, by type, along with the average number of members participating in meetings (not all student members attended or reported interventions for each meeting). The data shows that, throughout the pilot program, students were actively intervening when others were bullied. Students in the program are clearly no longer bystanders.

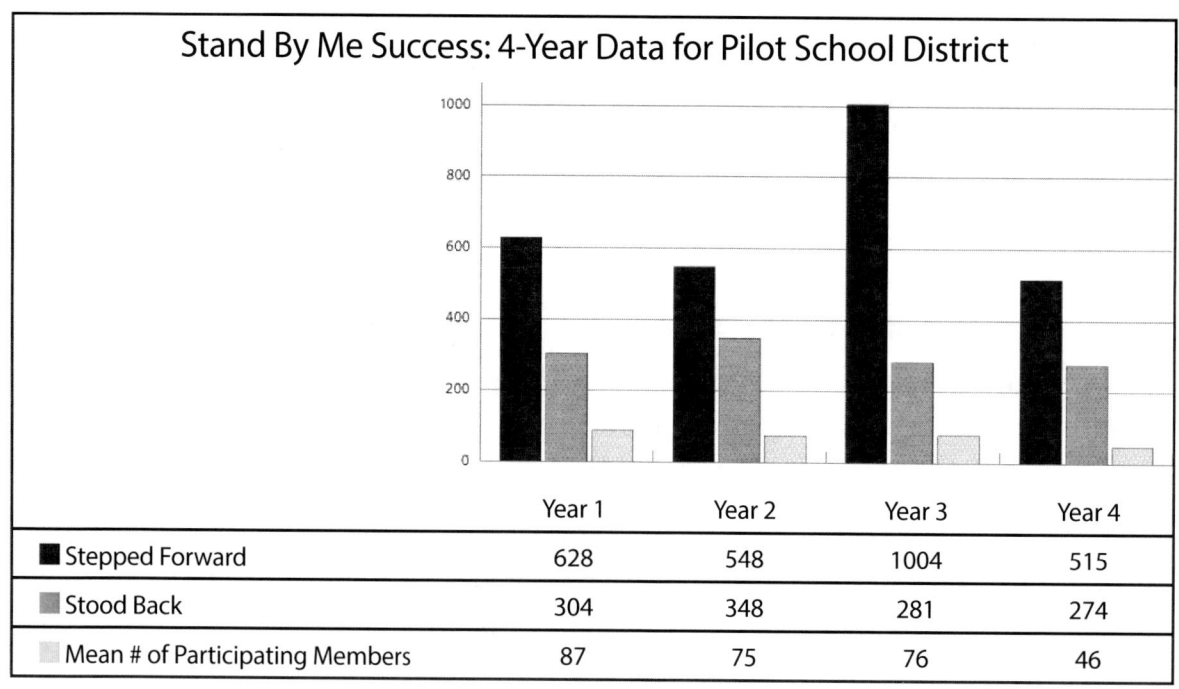

	Year 1	Year 2	Year 3	Year 4
■ Stepped Forward	628	548	1004	515
■ Stood Back	304	348	281	274
■ Mean # of Participating Members	87	75	76	46

First-Year Data for New School District

In 2012, the program was started in an additional district and followed for the first year. The data shows that not only were student bystanders active but that even with a small beginning membership, intervention numbers were quite high. The program rapidly showed results. (Please note that meetings in May were less frequent due to end-of-year activities.)

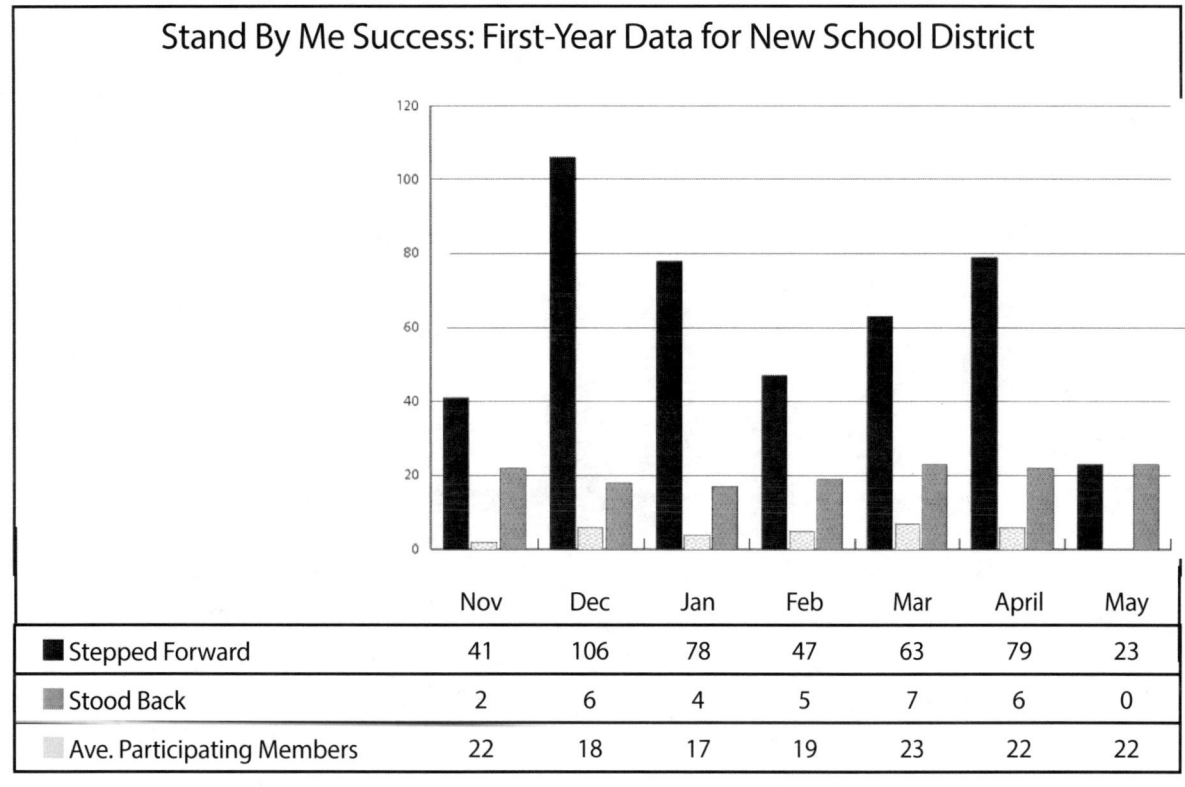

Stand By Me Success: First-Year Data for New School District

	Nov	Dec	Jan	Feb	Mar	April	May
■ Stepped Forward	41	106	78	47	63	79	23
■ Stood Back	2	6	4	5	7	6	0
■ Ave. Participating Members	22	18	17	19	23	22	22

3.

INTRODUCTION

Most kids like to go to school. Most kids have friends, find their niche, get involved in activities, and begin honing their interests. Even though status among peers is important, kids tend to work out status within their own circle of friends or interests. In other words, kids may not be cheerleaders, star athletes, or valedictorians, but they may be enviable artists, good writers, or natural comics.

Without the buffer of a peer group, school can be a lonely and even frightening place. Any student can become the target of bullying, including students who are emotionally fragile, physically or socially awkward, new to the school, have disabilities (both visible and invisible), female, LGBTQ, younger, or simply in the wrong place at the wrong time. Bullying typically occurs unobserved by staff and in places where students have no protection except what they can do for themselves to fight back.

STAND BY ME enlists peers because peers see bullying happen. Bullies try to draw in bystanders and feel reinforced by the attention and notoriety they attract. It is a rough but alternate route to peer leadership and status. Being either famous or infamous pays off in many of the same ways. STAND BY ME uses behavior principles to stop this behavior. The program competes for the bystanders. By attending to and removing the victim, while ignoring the bully, STAND BY ME participants work to extinguish bullying while modeling alternative behavior patterns for the bystanders. They remove the audience by removing the "show."

The result is that from the first day a student walks into the building he or she has a support system. Ultimately, as students become the recipients of this support, they may want to become a part of it. They are pulled into a caring community. Comments received from the victims are rewarding and affirming for the participants. Typical is one student comment to a member that, "You don't know how much of a good friend you've made … how much one person can change another person's life!"

The goal of STAND BY ME is to be inclusive, not exclusive – to create a campus culture that is supportive, protective, and that models good social skills. It offers everyone an opportunity for acceptance and leadership.

This book offers everything needed by a school district to implement this program, including the training of faculty sponsors.

The STAND BY ME Program differs from other bully-prevention programs in that it:

- Involves student bystanders
- Ignores the bully
- Removes the audience and, therefore, the reinforcing power of attention
- Provides an immediate support system for the victim
- Is simple and easy to train (training time for students is approximately 1 hour)
- Gives weekly data to school administrators, allowing them to assign staff to areas of greatest need
- Provides all students (including the bullies) a path to leadership and full membership in the school community

4.

PROGRAM OVERVIEW

- The program begins with an assembly to talk about a new anti-bullying program and a contest to design a school logo to represent the program. This graphic is featured on badges worn by the students to designate membership. Membership is voluntary and designed to include, rather than exclude, students.

- Students apply to be members and go through an interview process. Everyone is accepted, but applicants with disciplinary problems are accepted under a provisional status (see page 39). These students must remain free of discipline referrals for six weeks to be full members. They can earn days off of that time through community service.

- Faculty sponsors train students (see page 45) to help the victim of bullying while ignoring the bully. They carry program badges and data collection cards to record interventions (see page 36). Provisional members attend all meetings, but do not receive badges until they become full members.

- Regular meetings – weekly or bimonthly, depending school schedules – are held with the faculty sponsor to collect data, discuss questions and concerns, and problem-solve (see page 55).

- Administrators receive data on where and when interventions have occurred to help them determine how to assign staff in common areas.

5.

PROGRAM SET-UP

All materials needed to implement the STAND BY ME program can be accessed at https://standbymeforschools.com/thankyou.

Program Components:

- Selection and training of faculty sponsor
- Training of administrators, faculty, and staff
- Campus-wide kick-off with a contest to design program logo
- Application process with interview
- Student training
- Weekly meetings (during school day) with faculty sponsor

Staff Responsibilities:

- Create application packets
- Collect applications and checking for completion
- Establish voting process for campus ID
- Make (and laminate) ID/t-shirts/buttons
- Conduct student interviews
- Train students
- Hold regularly scheduled meetings (weekly is recommended) with faculty sponsor and students to analyze data
- Report data to administration
- Review of data by campus administrators
- Send campus data to STAND BY ME

6.

WHICH STUDENTS PARTICIPATE?

Student applicants come from a broad spectrum of the student body and include students who have been bullied, students who have bullied, students who are popular and students who are outsiders.

> "When I was in 5th and 6th grade, I was nothing but trouble. I went to [the disciplinary campus] four times. The first of this year I had four Fs on my report card. Now I'm on the AB honor roll."
> Kevin, 7th grade

> "The reason we're in the program is that we all used to do a lot of bullying and we feel bad. We also have been bullied and know what others are going through." Lakin, 7th grade

> "In the past, I've been bullied a lot and I see people bullied a lot, and I just want to put a stop to it, 'cause there's no need for it, really." Jacob, 5th grade

> "I don't like seeing kids bullied, 'cause in my life I've been bullied. It makes me hurt on the inside. I don't want other kids to go through it. I want to make a difference. I have been able to stand up to kids without backing down. I'll do whatever I'm instructed, but I want to help." Gaubriella, 6th grade

"A lot of people on my hall, people pick on them. I don't want people talking about me like that." Mikosha, 6th grade

"Sometimes, when I see people getting bullied, it really hurts, 'cause it makes me feel how they feel." Markiara, 5th grade

"A boy came to me and asked me if I wanted to steal a game in the teacher's desk. I said 'No' and he went and stole it, and afterward, he went back and showed it to his friends. All his friends laughed at me because I didn't steal the game and called me chicken." Mark, 5th grade

"I care about people. I don't want to see friends get in trouble. If friends need help, I help solve problems. I try to ignore people when they yell at me." Chris, 7th grade

7.

FACULTY SPONSOR'S ROLE

The faculty sponsor has a major role in the success of the program. The sponsor must help the students organize, keep the level of excitement up, make sure the program guidelines are followed, and emphasize recruitment. Although there is an application process, this is not to exclude students, but to ensure that those who join are motivated enough to complete the paperwork. The goal is to change the campus culture through continuously increasing student numbers and involvement.

The faculty sponsor must also support the students in the problem-solving process. Giving students adult solutions to the problems they experience will shut them down. Creating their own solutions, on the other hand, will energize them. It is their program.

> At one elementary campus, STAND BY ME students sponta-
> neously applauded when provisional members earned their
> badges.

Everyone must work to bring all students together and remain focused on their common goal: ending bullying.

Students also like recognition and acknowledgment. One elementary STAND BY ME group was asked to partner with students from their campus who were participating in Special Olympics. Students also held end-of-the-year picnics, donut breakfasts, and pizza parties. A group of elementary students presented the program, along with role plays of actual situations, to the school board. STAND BY ME members from the middle school visited an elementary school to discuss bullying and the program. Students participating in the program also asked to have adults they admired in the school district and community come and speak with them about their own paths to success in life.

For students, the most difficult part of the program is data collection. The sponsor must make sure students turn in data every week. Lost badges have also been an ongoing problem, so it may be helpful to set up a place where students can pick them up each day, and then return them at the end of the day.

Finally, it is important to involve the students in the training process when new recruits come in.

8.

TRAINING OF ADMINISTRATORS, FACULTY, AND STAFF

"The fourth person I helped … really made me feel good. I introduced myself and walked him to class. Before he walked in the door of his class, he said, 'You don't know how much of a good friend you've made … how much one person can change another's life!'" Middle school STAND BY ME member

All campus staff should be trained in the program before implementation begins. STAND BY ME requires students to act in ways that may be at odds with school routines. For example, many schools have assigned cafeteria seating. STAND BY ME requires students to get up and assist other students, sit with them if necessary, or invite students to sit at their table. Staff needs to understand and allow this.

Staff training can occur in 20–30 minutes during a regular staff meeting. Staff must be made aware of program guidelines, such as:

1. Membership logos may be accepted instead of tardy slips.
2. Students may change tables in the cafeteria.
3. Students do not "name names" or turn in bullies.
4. The time and day when STAND BY ME meetings are held.

Print or copy at least ten High Five Cards (see page 58) for each teacher/staff member. Staff should each be given 10 High Five Cards and understand when to give them out.

Emphasize the fact that STAND BY ME students do not reveal the names of bullies. The staff needs to understand this so that students are not pressed to do so. In addition, staff must accept tardies with badges and be able to give out the High Five Cards cards.

A handout for administrator, faculty and staff appears on the following page.

FACULTY INFORMATION SHEET

STAND BY ME is a peer support program designed to address bullying. It trains student bystanders to assist the victims of bullying by knowing when and how to intervene. Students do not turn in bullies, but give information to administrators on where and how frequently bullying is occurring. The program is designed to be used for fifth through eighth grades.

The following is critical information you need in order to support these students:

- Each student in the program will wear an ID badge. If program members see a victim of bullying, they are taught to introduce themselves, provide support to the victim, and walk him or her to class.

- If students are late to your class because of an intervention, they must present their ID badge and should be admitted without a tardy.

- If student members help a victim in the cafeteria, they may be allowed to move to the victim's table or invite the victim to their table.

- Students are trained to ignore the bully. The members report information to administration monthly about the number of interventions and where they are occurring. They do not report the names of the bullies!!! If they are asked for names, they are taught to tell the questioning adult that they are in the STAND BY ME program and that they do not name names.

- Students are taught not to intervene when there is physical aggression, but instead to alert an adult as to what is occurring and where.

- If you see a student intervening in a case of physical aggression, or if you know a student is abusing the ID badge privilege (e.g., to talk with a friend), please report this to the faculty sponsors.

- Special issue regarding discipline referrals: High Five Cards will be given to all staff members. Students who are working to earn their STAND BY ME ID logo may be awarded High Five Cards for community service or helping school students or staff. Each card is worth one day off of the six weeks they must be discipline-free to earn their badge.

- If you have additional students who are interested in the program, please ask them to apply by contacting the sponsors. If you have any questions or concerns, you may direct them to the sponsor(s) or to your campus administrators.

Data has shown that once taught how to help, STAND BY ME members do help, having made over 4,000 interventions in 4 years. These are the kinds of numbers that can make a difference. Please support our members as they work to support each other.

9.

GETTING STARTED

1. Introducing the STAND BY ME Program: Membership Drive and Design Contest for Campus Badge

2. Application Process

3. Interview

4. Discipline Review

5. Letters of Acceptance

Introducing the STAND BY ME Program to Your Campus

The first step is to talk with your students about the program. This can occur through a whole-campus assembly or visiting individual classrooms. At this time, applications are distributed to all students who express interest in the STAND BY ME program. Initially, an administrator, counselor, or teacher/sponsor may do this, but after the program has been going for a year, students already in the program can assist with the presentation.

The introduction should emphasize key program components and that you want students who can do things that are not always easy. Here are some sample points:

- We are starting a new program to stop bullying on campus. We are your faculty sponsors.

- How many of you have been teased or bullied? How many have seen bullying happen?

  STAND BY ME teaches you what to do when you see bullying happen and how to help the victim.

- We don't name names or turn people in.

- We want students who are willing to make difficult decisions and stand up when their friends may not.

- We will meet every week. Meetings will take place during the school day, so you do not have to worry about transportation.

- We are kicking off the program with a design contest for our logo. The student who has the winning design will get

  _____.

- Applications must be turned in to _____ by _____ [date].

Introduce the design contest to come up with a recognizable logo for tags/buttons/t-shirts and all other program forms, such as badges. Doing this will generate excitement about the program.

Not all students will complete a design. That's okay because it is not required. Once the application deadline is past, all submitted designs should be posted in a common area of the school for EVERYONE on campus (not just applicants) to vote on. They should be posted anonymously. This can be done by folding them in half and assigning numbers to each design. Teachers should make sure their classes are taken past the designs to view them all and turn in class votes to STAND BY ME sponsors.

The winner should be announced and should receive a prize, such as a gift certificate.

Students should wear the graphic in some form as an identifier of membership. This can be part of their laminated hall pass, a button, t-shirt, etc. Because this is a student-run program, the students at a given campus can decide how to signify membership.

The logo contest entry form (see page 40) is attached to the application packet. Following the initial school presentation, packets should be passed out in classes, with teachers responsible for collecting completed application forms and returning them to a central point. Again, application is voluntary, not required.

Application Process

The application is a multi-part packet that includes:

- Introductory Letter from Campus Administrators for educational professionals

- Student Application Form

- Letter of Recommendation

- Parent/Guardian Permission to Participate Form

- Parent/Guardian Permission to View Website Form

- Design Your Logo Contest

As applications are returned, set up a database of student names. Check to see if all components are completed, especially parent permission to participate (the graphic design is optional). The most common problem is students having friends or siblings complete their letter of recommendation. If they do this, simply give them another recommendation form for an adult to complete. If they do not know who to approach, brainstorm ideas with them (e.g., teacher, neighbor) or offer to go with them to ask an adult.

Once applications are complete (i.e., they must include recommendations and parent permission), students are eligible for the interview.

APPLICATION PACKET

PROGRAM DESCRIPTION

Goals: Prevent/reduce incidents of teasing and bullying

Develop leadership skills

Create an immediate support system for victims of teasing and bullying

Program Description

The STAND BY ME program is a simple way for students to show their support for peers who are teased and bullied. It provides opportunities for practicing leadership skills and creates a vehicle for discussing teasing and bullying on student campuses.

Any student may apply, and there is no limit on the number of students who can participate.

Student participants are trained by staff and receive an identifying logo to wear.

Participants go through their normal daily schedules and routines at school, but if they hear or observe someone being teased or bullied, their job is to stand by that person and/or offer to walk with them to their destination. If the incident occurs in the cafeteria, they should offer to sit with the student. Members should not say anything to the student bullying, or try to intervene; their role is to stay with the target student, chat with him/her, and offer support. Once they have accompanied that student to his/her destination, or when the bullying has stopped, they should report to their next scheduled class. Members use their badge as a hall pass to show if they are tardy to class because they were assisting a student. They do not report the bully – their goal is to demonstrate support for the target student and thereby draw attention away from the student or students causing the problem.

As more and more students become involved in the program, the logo will serve a visual reminder to ALL students that they are members of a campus that does not support bullies.

Student members log the number of times they assist a student and the location where they provided assistance so that campus administrators can keep data on the number of incidents and assign staff more effectively, as needed.

Members attend regular meetings with their faculty sponsor to discuss their experiences, get peer support, and evaluate program success.

_____   _____

Principal   Faculty Sponsor

APPLICATION CHECKLIST

U   Student Application Form

U   Letter of Recommendation

U   Parent/Guardian Permission to Participate Form

U   Parent/Guardian Permission to View Website Form

U   STAND BY ME Design Your Logo Contest

STUDENT APPLICATION FORM

Name: _____ Grade:_____

Address: _____

Parent/Guaridan Name(s): _____

Contact Phone: _____

Teacher: _____

Please attach a letter of recommendation from an adult who knows you well
(coach, teacher, neighbor, scout leader, etc.).

_____

The STAND BY ME program wants students who show outstanding qualities of
leadership – students who are independent thinkers and who are not afraid to
"go against the crowd" when they make decisions. If you think this describes
you, please answer the following questions.

1. Describe a time when you have felt peer pressure to do something you knew was
   wrong. Tell what you did and why. How did your friends treat you afterward?

   _____
   _____
   _____

2. Define "leadership." What is the difference between a good leader and a
   bad leader?

   _____
   _____
   _____

3. Who is a role model in your life and why? _____

   _____
   _____
   _____
   _____

LETTER OF RECOMMENDATION

Student Name: _____

How do you know this student? How long have you known him/her?

_____
_____
_____
_____

What talents or abilities do you feel this student will bring to the program?

_____
_____
_____
_____

How well does the student get along with peers? Adults?

_____
_____
_____
_____

What else do you think we should know about this student?

_____
_____
_____

Please sign here: Please put the date here:

_____   _____

Please print your name here:

_____

PARENT/GUARDIAN PERMISSION TO PARTICIPATE FORM

I hereby give my permission for my child, _____, to participate in the STAND BY ME program. I understand that he/she will receive training on program guidelines and procedures and will work with faculty/staff sponsors.

I also agree to my child's participation in training and, although all regular meetings will take place during the school day, I will provide transportation so that my child may attend training and any after-school meetings, if needed. I understand that such participation is required for the STAND BY ME program.

_____   _____
Parent/Guardian signature   Date

_____
Please print your name here

PARENT/GUARDIAN PERMISSION TO VIEW WEBSITE

Dear Parent/Guardian:

A STAND BY ME website is an active part of our program. It features postings by student groups as well as a gallery of STAND BY ME member artwork. The website gives STAND BY ME campus groups the ability to post articles, stories, ideas, photos, etc. All postings will be reviewed and approved by the STAND BY ME faculty sponsor and be consistent with district policy regarding such postings. Postings will be uploaded only by the faculty sponsor or campus administrator. Individual students will have viewing access only.

Please indicate below whether we have your permission to use your son or daughter's contributions and artwork on the website. All individual work will be identified only by first name, grade, and campus.

Although this release is not required for membership, we encourage you to allow your son or daughter to participate in this part of the program. You may view the Stand By Me website at https://standbymeforschools.com

Very truly yours,

_____   _____
Campus Administrator   Faculty Sponsor

_____   _____   _____
Student Name   Grade   Campus

_____   _____   _____
Parent/Guardian Signature   Parent/Guardian Name (Printed)   Date

RELEASE: Please check one

U   You have my permission to post my son/daughter's individual work identified by first name, grade, and campus.

U   You DO NOT have my permission to post my son/daughter's work.

DESIGN YOUR LOGO CONTEST!

OUR NEW STAND BY ME PROGRAM IS LOOKING FOR AN OUTSTANDING DESIGN FOR THE BADGES TO BE WORN BY ITS MEMBERS!

THE WINNER WILL RECEIVE _____.

RULES:

- All entries must be submitted to _____ by the end of the school day on _____.
- All entries must be submitted on this official form and be limited to the size of the space below.
- Only one entry per student.
- All entries must be consistent with school rules and the Student Code of Conduct.

NAME: _____   GRADE: _____

END OF APPLICATION PACKET

INTERVIEW GUIDELINES

The interview, which typically brief, is where the STAND BY ME training truly begins. Most students have never been interviewed like this and naturally feel some anxiety. Part of the purpose of the interview is for students to begin practicing what the program requires of them: to put themselves in a situation that makes them anxious and nevertheless do what is necessary. At least two adults should be present, the faculty sponsor and either a counselor or an administrator. Some of the most effective interviews have consisted of a three-adult panel, but due to time constraints, this may not always be practical.

The setting should be formal, and the student should sit across the table from the adults. The adults should have read the student's application and begin by making some positive comments about the student's answers or the recommendation letters. It is also appropriate to reassure the student that there are no right or wrong answers; the student is just to answer honestly.

Components of the interview include:

- Reviewing the application and recommendation letters before the student comes in.

- Welcoming the student and introducing the adults.

- Beginning with a positive comment about students' paperwork, such as "You had some strong answers to the questions we asked" or "You had a really good recommendation."

- Asking students if they have read their own letter of recommendation. Most often they have not, so it is helpful to read an excerpt that says something special about them.

- Asking the interview questions (see page 38).

- Encouraging students to respond, by telling them there are no wrong answers. Students will respond in very different ways. Some will be confident and articulate, whereas others will be very shy and have a hard time saying anything. If a student speaks too softly, for example, ask her to speak louder and praise her for doing so.

- Telling students, at the conclusion of the interview, that you will be completing all the interviews before making a decision, but that you hope they are successful because you think they will make a great addition to the program. You can also tell students that you think they handled themselves well and gave good answers. Your positive comments will help give students confidence in their ability to handle difficult situations and make it more likely that they will be willing to do so in the future.

INTERVIEW QUESTIONS

Student's Name: _____ Date: _____

1. What skills and/or talents do you possess that will benefit the STAND BY ME program?

    _____

    _____

    _____

2. Describe the last time you had to stop yourself from saying or doing something that you really wanted to say or do.

    _____

    _____

    _____

3. Describe what bullying looks like to you.

    _____

    _____

    _____

4. Have you ever been bullied or bullied others?

    _____

    _____

    _____

5. What keeps students from speaking out or helping others when they see bullying?

    _____

    _____

    _____

DISCIPLINE REVIEW

Once interviews are completed, applications are reviewed and checked against discipline referrals. All students are accepted, but some are accepted provisionally. All acceptance letters welcome the student into the program and give the time and date of the training, along with the training guidelines.

Students who have had no discipline referrals within the past six weeks receive a standard acceptance letter. They go through training, receive their member badge (which allows them to perform interventions) and attend meetings.

Students who have received a discipline referral within the past six weeks receive a letter of provisional acceptance, go through training, and attend meetings. However, they do not receive their member badge (which allows them to perform interventions) until their discipline record has been clean for six weeks.

Provisional acceptance is usually not an issue if the initial recruitment drive occurs at the beginning of the school year. However, the program is ongoing with applications being submitted throughout the year, so it is an issue that may occur.

The provisional letter states that students must be free of discipline referrals for six weeks before receiving their membership badges, but that they may attend all meetings and activities. These students receive calendars rather than badges at the initial meeting, showing the number of days left until they can receive badges. They will have the opportunity to earn High Five Cards through community service for days off of the six-week period.

Students who receive discipline referrals after getting their membership badges may lose their badges for up to six weeks. Decisions about penalties may be made jointly between the sponsor and the assistant principal (see sample problem solving).

Before badges are given out, find an opportunity to talk with any provisional members one-on-one to explain that they will receive a calendar rather than a badge. Tell them also about their opportunity to earn High Five Cards for days off the six-week waiting period; for example, by speaking in front of the group about their experience.

At your initial meeting introduce this practice to the entire STAND BY ME group:

> "Because everyone must be free from discipline referrals for 6 weeks in order to earn their badges, we have some members who will receive badges at a later date. Because we support each other, and because we applaud the courage it takes to admit mistakes, these members have the opportunity to complete community service to earn High Five tickets from teachers.
>
> For every High Five Card they earn, they will receive one day off of that six weeks waiting period. If you are committed to supporting them, you can help them on their projects, and encourage their efforts.
>
> In fact, if anyone working on their badge would like to come up and talk about what they did to get their discipline referral, and what they plan to do differently the next time, they can earn five cards, or a week off of their 6-week time, here at the meeting."

If any students volunteer, be sure they get a show of support from the group.

ACCEPTANCE LETTER

Dear _____:

Congratulations! You have been chosen to participate in our new STAND BY ME anti-bullying program. We based our selection of students on their good leadership skills and strong desire to help others. You met that standard and impressed us with your application and interview.

Attached are copies of the training guidelines that we will cover together. Please give a copy to your parent/guardian(s) so they will also be familiar with the program procedures.

We are very excited to have you in our program, and look forward to seeing you during training on _____.

Sincerely,

_____   _____

Principal   Faculty Sponsor

PROVISIONAL ACCEPTANCE LETTER

Dear _____:

Thank you for applying to be part of the STAND BY ME program. You had a strong application and interview. The only obstacle to your acceptance into the program is that you have one or more discipline referrals. We believe you have the leadership qualities it takes to overcome this and hope you will participate as follows:

> You will be trained and attend STAND BY ME meetings with the other members. You will help track the data collected by members. You will also participate in solving problems, making posters, recruiting new members, and any other group activities.

> You will not yet have a member badge to make interventions. HOWEVER, if you can go six weeks without a discipline referral (dated from the time of your last referral), you will receive your badge and become a fully participating member.

We hope you will strongly consider this option, as we think you have the strengths and skills to make the program even better. We need many kinds of support, and all of us working together, to solve the bullying problem.

Sincerely,

_____   _____

Principal   Faculty Sponsor

10.

STAND BY ME TRAINING PROCESS

Handouts for the Training Process

- Training Guidelines and Rules to Remember (see page 46)
- Student Data Card (see page 50)
- Laminated set of Role-Plays for Training (see page 47)

Once the faculty sponsor has become thoroughly familiar with the program, s/he can train students. The training process continues what began in the interview: Students learn to stand up by doing just that with an audience of their peers.

Student training takes about 30–45 minutes. Depending on the number of members, you may want to train grade levels separately. It is good to keep the group to 25 or 30 students. Require students to stand up to answer questions and to repeat if they are not loud enough or not clearly understood. In addition, students should be thanked for doing these things.

The training begins with an interactive discussion of some of the issues talked about in the interview (e.g., what is bullying and how do you know it when you see it?) Each time students raise their hand, they have to stand up and give their answer. If they do not speak loudly enough, ask them, in an encouraging way, to repeat their answer (e.g., "That was a great answer! Say it again so everyone can hear."). Throughout the training, always reinforce students standing up and participating with lots of praise and positive comments. Also reinforce the students praising and making positive comments to each other.

Training consists of the following:
- Review Training Guidelines and Rules to Remember.
- Emphasize "know when to step forward" and "know when to stand back."
- Teach use of the data card.
- Review reasons for dismissal from the program.
- Practice problem-solving situations (role-plays for training).
- Remind students of time and day of the first meeting.
- Optional: Hand out member badges and calendars (for students who are provisional members, due to discipline issues) or wait until the first meeting.
- Beginning after the initial recruitment drive, members may be asked to assist with the training.
- Distribute handouts (see next section)
    1. Review the Training Guidelines (page x) and Rules to Remember (page x) and explain the Student Data Card. STAND BY ME members are trained for two kinds of interventions: "Stepping Forward," which means they help a victim directly, and "Standing Back," which means that there is physical aggression involved, so they alert an adult instead.
    2. Assign each student a number from 1-7. For example, if you have 21 students in the group, you will have three sets of students numbered 1-7.
    3. Group the students by number (all the 1s, 2s, etc.) and give each group a laminated role-play card. Give them a few minutes to discuss and come up with a group solution to the role-play. Have each group present and explain their solution. Remind the students that the guidelines are for STAND BY ME members acting on behalf of a victim. STAND BY ME members are not required or even asked to report the bully, but the victims themselves are always free to do so.
- End the training by answering questions and giving the date and time of the first meeting.

TRAINING GUIDELINES

- If there is fighting, DO NOT stay. Leave immediately and notify an adult.
- Do not talk with or respond to the bully. You are there to pay attention to the student who is the target. The bully is invisible as far as you are concerned.
- Give your name. You do not need to ask the target student's name at first. Just say, "Hi, my name is _____. Where are you headed? I'll walk with you." The target student may be embarrassed or upset, and may not want to talk.
- If the student does not want to walk with you, you can just stand with her for a few minutes and talk to her. You can even just stand quietly and keep the student company. It is okay to give the student some space, if needed.
- If you are in the cafeteria, introduce yourself and ask if you can sit with the student for a minute. If the bully is at the student's table, you can introduce yourself and ask the student if he would like to change tables and sit with you.
- If you are outside, introduce yourself and suggest that you walk together. Then move toward the nearest adult and away from the bully. If there is a crowd, let an adult know that bullying is going on.
- Do not walk into any situation that makes you uncomfortable.

Remember, you are not there to report the names of bullies, You are there to support the target student!

KNOW WHEN TO STEP FORWARD!
KNOW WHEN TO STAND BACK!

Remember to be an example of:
LEADERSHIP
SERVICE
SELF-CONTROL

RULES TO REMEMBER

- Help the victim ignore the bully.
- Do not name names.
- If there is fighting or physical contact, do not stay! Go to the nearest adult and tell him/her what is happening and where. If the adult asks who is involved, say that you are in the STAND BY ME program and that you do not report names.
- If you are in class or there is a teacher present, let the teacher handle the situation.
- Use your badge if you are late to class ONLY if you have helped someone.
- On your STAND BY ME card, keep track of times you help.

You can be dismissed for:

- Not following these rules.
- Using your badge for tardies when you have not made a STAND BY ME intervention.
- Receiving discipline referrals.

ROLE-PLAYS FOR TRAINING
(STUDENT COPY)

1. You are walking to class and see a student run past another student, knocking his books out of his hands in the process.

2. You are outside before school and hear several students name-calling another student.

3. You are in the cafeteria. A student walks by another student at a nearby table and grabs her dessert.

4. You are in the hallway and see a student pushing another student up against the wall.

5. You are in class and hear two students talking about "jumping" a third student after school.

6. You are in class. The teacher is in the hall, monitoring traffic. Two girls begin to tease another girl who puts her head down on her desk, clearly upset.

7. You are in class. One student jumps up, yells a profanity, and shoves another student's papers onto the floor.

ROLE-PLAYS FOR TRAINING
(TRAINER'S COPY)

1. You are walking to class and see a student run past another student, knocking his books out of his hands in the process.

   • Go to the student who lost his books, introduce yourself, and ask if you can walk with him to class. Help him retrieve his books.

2. You are outside before school and hear several students name-calling another student.

   • Go to the student, introduce yourself and see if he will walk with you. Walk toward the nearest adult. Ignore the students who are calling names.

3. You are in the cafeteria. A student walks by another student at a nearby table and grabs her dessert.

   • Go to the student who has lost her dessert, introduce yourself, and ask if you can sit with her or if she would like to sit with you at your table. Offer to share your dessert with her.

4. You are in the hallway and see a student pushing another student up against the wall.

   • In this case, you do not intervene because there is physical contact and aggression. Instead, go to the nearest adult and report a fight at that location. Do not identify the bully, only the event and its location.

5. You are in class and hear two students talking about "jumping" a third student after school.

   • This involves planned physical aggression. Report the conversation to staff along with the time and location, if known. You can identify the potential victim if you have a name or description.

6. You are in class. The teacher is at the door, monitoring both the classroom and hall traffic. Two girls begin to tease another girl who puts her head down on her desk, clearly upset.

   - Follow your teacher's directives for beginning class. Your teacher is present, and it is her class. Allow her to intervene. You could introduce yourself to the student after class, offer to walk with her to her next class and, perhaps, meet her before your shared class the next day.

7. You are in class. One student jumps up, yells profanity, and shoves another student's papers onto the floor.

   - As a STAND BY ME member, you do not intervene in a case of physical aggression. Nor do you intervene when staff is present and observing the event. But you can offer to assist the student in picking up his belongings if the teacher allows.

DATA CARDS
FOR ELEMENTARY AND SECONDARY STUDENTS

The data card can be formatted to reflect individual campuses and schedules. For elementary students, the card should be laminated to the back of their hall pass/ID card. For secondary students, the data cards can simply be paper slips clipped to a folder or notebook.

Data cards are to be turned in (for secondary students) or counted (for elementary students) each week at the meetings. Students at all grade levels should help compile data.

ELEMENTARY DATA CARD PROCEDURES

Items needed: Elementary Card

Elementary students receive red and green mini dot stickers to "park" on the bottom of their badges. Each time they help a victim, they put a green sticker in the "Stepped Forward" column in the appropriate location. Each time they observe an incident of bullying in which they did not intervene, they put a red sticker in the "Stood Back" column in the appropriate location.

ELEMENTARY CARD SAMPLE

Stepped Forward	Stood Back
Hall	
Restroom	
Gym	
Cafeteria	
Outside	
Park your dots	Park your dots

PROCEDURES FOR SECONDARY STUDENTS

Items needed: Badge/data card (see data card directions below)

- Badge: Wear your identifier at all times in school.

- Data Card: Every time you help a target student, put a mark on your card noting the time and location. Each week bring your data card to our meeting to turn in. Add any notes you feel are relevant or important. If you lose your data card, you can pick up another from your faculty sponsor or the front office. You must show your STAND BY ME badge in order to get a data card.

- If you are late to class because you have stopped to help a student, present your badge to your teacher to be admitted to class.

IMPORTANT!

Being in this program is a privilege. You can be dismissed from the program for the following reasons:

- Using your hall pass inappropriately (e.g., using it when you are late without having stopped to help a student).

- Behaving in a way that is outside the training guidelines. You will get warnings and opportunities to correct mistakes, but if you do not conform to training guidelines after that time, you will be dismissed.

FACULTY SPONSOR

- _____ is your faculty sponsor. If you have any questions or concerns between meetings, this teacher is your contact.

SECONDARY DATA CARD PROCEDURES

SECONDARY CARD SAMPLE

Period	0	1	2	3	A.P.	Lunch	4	5	6	7	0
Hall 1 B											
Hall 2 B											
Hall 1 C											
Hall 2 C											
Hall A											
Cafeteria											
Gym											
Outside											
Restroom											
Library											
Foyer 1											
Foyer 2											

Name:_____ Date:_____

Notes: _____

_____

_____

_____

Mark a "1" each time you helped a student. Mark a "0" each time you saw a problem but did not help for any reason (e.g., there was fighting, or you were uncomfortable getting involved).

11.

STAND BY ME STUDENT MEETINGS

General Procedures

Regular meetings are crucial for keeping enthusiasm going. It is important to remember that this is a student-led program. Challenge students to solve the problems they encounter as a result of participating in the program. Continually emphasize that they are the ones who need to problem-solve. Typically, if an adult tries to run things, the students shut down. Students should be guided in discussing difficult situations they have encountered, suggestions to administrators for solving bullying issues in the building, how to support each other, new initiatives for the program, how to recruit more members, and what they would like to do during meetings.

All meetings should have a high degree of student participation. Students need to track the number of interventions, the locations, and the times to help them see progress and solve future problems that arise. Data is entered on the weekly summary form, and student comments or suggestions are added as the meeting continues.

Meeting agenda should include:
- Sign in
- Report data and summarize
- Issue High Five Cards
- Discuss the week's issues and have students make suggestions for administrators
- Recruiting ideas (e.g., posters, STAND BY ME buddies)
- Read STAND BY ME stories

Once the data is collected, the meeting can be opened up to the students for reports on how the week has gone, any problems that have occurred, possible solutions, and working through any questions or confusion about the intervention process. Other possibilities for meeting agendas include:

- Setting up the STAND BY ME Story box (see Chapter 12)
- Having guest speakers (e.g., principal, superintendent, favorite teacher, parent, community leaders)
- Creating a blog post for the STAND BY ME website
- Discussing requests from parents or staff for a STAND BY ME buddy
- Participating in school or community service projects, such as assisting with Special Olympics

It is important to push the students to be the problem solvers and not impose adult ideas on them. This shuts the process down. The adult is there to facilitate and maintain enthusiasm to help and encourage the members to bring other students into the program.

STAND BY ME Website

The STAND BY ME website (standbymeforschools.com) was created, in part, as a way to share program successes and problem-solving ideas; to generate a continuous stream of data; and to create a wider on-line community that supports the individual school communities participating in the program. It is designed as a forum to post logos, ideas, and to collaborate. It is also a resource for training. Your school or community organization can access all forms needed to implement the STAND BY ME program (including application packets and student training materials).

All posting to the website must be approved and uploaded by the faculty sponsor. All faculty sponsors are assigned log-in information using instructions on the website. Student members should submit ideas or posts to the sponsor, who then makes sure that content is appropriate and district policies regarding confidentiality are followed. A sample consent form for online posting is available in the forms link on the website.

Posting should include all STAND BY ME data generated by your member groups. This can be submitted through the designated website link (https://standbymeforschools.com/thankyou). The continuing review of data will help to improve programming and track program success.

It is another way for us all to stand together to defeat bullying.

High Five Cards

Students working off discipline referrals receive High Five cards for helping teachers and staff, or doing some kind of community service. Each card represents one day off the six weeks they must be free of discipline referrals. Teachers and staff receive a supply of cards to hand out to the students. Students turn in the High Five Cards at meetings. Students with calendars get one High Five Card each week for coming to meetings.

WEEKLY SUMMARY REPORT FOR ADMINISTRATORS

The Weekly Summary Report is a compilation of the student data gathered at each meeting. Part of the meeting procedure involves reviewing and tallying interventions from the student data cards. After data is collected, the students clear their cards, so they are ready to be reused. Depending on student age, the report can be completed by the faculty sponsor or the students in conjunction with the sponsor. Once completed, it is to be turned in to the designated campus administrator.

Sample Weekly Summary Report

Campus:

Date:

Period	0	1	2	3	A.P.	Lunch	4	5	6	7	0	Stair	Total
Hall 1 B													
Hall 2 B													
Hall 1 C													
Hall 2 C													
Hall A													
Cafeteria													
Gym													
Outside													
Restroom													
Library													
Foyer 1													
Foyer 2													
Total													

Numbers represent STAND BY ME Interventions. Each "0" represents an incidence of fighting or an incident in which a STAND BY ME student did not feel comfortable intervening for any reason.

Total interventions:_____

Total incidents observed without intervention (fighting, etc.):_____

Number of students reporting:_____

MEETING NOTES

Student Ideas and Observations
(copy to be sent with data summary to administrators)

_____

_____

_____

_____

_____

_____

_____

_____

_____

_____

_____

_____

_____

_____

_____

_____

_____

_____

_____

_____   _____

Student   Sponsor

_____

Date

SAMPLES OF STUDENT MEETINGS

The program is designed to be run by students. In weekly meetings with a faculty sponsor, students are challenged to solve the problems they have encountered as members of the program. Below are samples of this process as reported in actual meetings.

Elementary School: 5th Grade

Problem: Fifth graders reported a new student who was bullying other kids. The members told the teachers what was happening.

Solution: Together, the sponsor and the members discussed ways to help the new student feel welcome, as well as how they could stand together to let him know that they did not tolerate bullying. The members voted on whether bullying has gotten better, stayed the same, or gotten worse. The majority said it was better. They said they were all feeling more confident about intervening in bullying situations.

Middle School:

Problem: "There are lots of restroom problems. Lots of fights there after school or in the hallway. All the teachers are in the cafeteria because of bus duty. Lots of times kids meet outside to fight behind the school in the big trees. They even jump people there. We've had to go and get teachers for fights in certain locations where there are no teachers around."

Solution: Students recorded the information on their data summary cards for administrators, along with suggestions for teacher locations.

Problem: "I was getting bullied this week. A big kid pushed me into the wall. I just ignored him and kept walking. Then he hit me in the back of the head with something that really hurt. I turned around and saw something metal in his hand. I didn't fight back. I went and sat in Coach's office until the student passed by."

Problem: "They hit me for being in the program. They think we're snitches. I got hit really hard in the head with a backpack. I still have a knot on my head."

Solution: The student solution was to design a business card to hand out with the program rules, including the fact that members do not identify bullies or name names. These cards were printed on card stock and laminated and distributed to all students.

Problem: "We need to have more people in the program."

Solution: The student solution was a recruiting drive, with target goals on posters around the campus. The students also put up "mystery signs" that read "SBM" and listed a number signifying the total number of interventions by STAND BY ME members. The signs were laminated and lettered with dry-erase markers so the numbers could be updated weekly.

Problem: The sponsor received excessive faculty reports that STAND BY ME member students were verbally harassing other students.

Solution: In order to address these issues, students established a new procedure. If a faculty sponsor learned that a member was verbally "bullying," the sponsor would call the person who recommended the harassing student and let him/her know. The next time the same member was involved in verbally harassing another, he would lose his badge for six weeks. Within a month, the harassment behaviors disappeared.

12.

GATHERING STAND BY ME STORIES

STAND BY ME stories are a way to share program experiences with members and other students. They are also a way to collect information to improve the program.

An anonymous collection box for STAND BY ME stories should be placed at a designated location (e.g., outside the faculty sponsor's classroom or at the front office) along with a supply of blank story forms. Students can complete the forms and place them in the box for collection by the faculty sponsor or a designated member.

STORIES

U   I helped someone

U   Someone helped me

Where? _____

_____

_____

_____

_____

When? _____

_____

_____

_____

_____

What happened? _____

_____

_____

_____

_____

13.

STAND BY ME STUDENT COMMENTS

(5th and 6th grade)

1. How has being in STAND BY ME changed your outlook on bullying?

    "Helping people is a good thing."

    "It encourages me to tell people not to bully or be mean to others, and inspires me to help others outside of school."

    "It makes you think how the little things can hurt people even if it is not intentionally."

    "It's having the card, because I could [go] by the fighting and help the person who got bullied."

    "People used to always be fighting, and now it is more calm."

    "I've seen what it looks like and I know that it hurts people."

    "It has changed a lot, like if I get bullied, I would know what to do and not fight them or something."

    "Because there is a lot of bullying, and we helped solve it."

    "It inspires me to stand up and talk to a person."

    "I can recognize more things as bullying."

"It encourages me to tell other people not to be mean."

"It stops a lot of bullying."

"I feel an obligation to say something."

2. Has the bullying problem in your school increased or decreased since the program began? Why or why not?"

    "The bullying has decreased because more teachers are in the hall and in problem areas."

    "It has decreased because more kids know what we do and know we are everywhere."

    "It has decreased because some kids stop when they know we're here."

    "I think it has decreased since there are many people to look out."

    "It has decreased because now I'm barely seeing fighting and bullying."

    "It has decreased because we are making marks [on our cards] of them and watching them."

3. What do you like about the program that you would like for us to continue next year?

    "I like how we keep a record on our badges."

    "I like helping people."

    "I like helping special education."

    "I like the meetings so you can decide things that need to be changed."

    "I like that we meet every week and we keep a record of the bullying."

    "I like that STAND BY ME got to help in the Special Olympics."

    "I would like to continue the pizza discussions [the end of the year wrap-up]."

"I like having the badge."

"We have caring people. People who care."

"I like that now that we have STAND BY ME, not that much fight[ing] has been happening."

"Well, I really like the people and for us to be in it again."

4. What would you like to change about the program for next year?

"Inform more people."

"Have pep rallies."

"Have hall monitors in the morning. Take turns serving as hall monitor."

"Have a monitor on every hall with different shifts."

"Do more at meetings."

"Have demonstrations (ongoing role-plays)."

"Assign one STAND BY ME member to each cafeteria table."

"Educate teachers about what they see."

"Inspire other kids."

"Have a rally to recruit new members."

"Add a classroom spot on the tag so we can identify bullying for other teachers."

"Go into classrooms and talk about STAND BY ME."

"Have a button or logo that hooks onto our shirts or backpacks to show we are members."

"Have a different design every year with a new contest."

"Maybe we could do more stuff like when we see a fight happen and we either stand back or stop it, we should be able to ask our teachers to talk to the students and see why they were fighting." [Members are not supposed to identify the students.]

"There has been a lot of improvement. I was helping three or four people when we started. Now I'm really just helping one."

Related Books from AAPC

Perfect Targets:

Asperger Syndrome and Bullying - Practical Solutions for Surviving the Social World

Rebekah Heinrichs, MSN, MSEd

Code 9918
Price: $19.95

Social Rules for Kids:

The Top 100 Social Rules Kids Need to Succeed

Susan Diamond, MA, CCC

Code 9067
Price: $19.95

Talk with Me:

A Step-by-Step Conversation Framework for Teaching Conversational Balance and Fluency for High-Functioning Individuals with Autism Spectrum Disorder

Kerry Mataya, MSEd, Ruth Aspy, PhD and Hollis Shaffer

Code 9140
Price: $21.95

The Secret Rules of Social Networking

Barbara Klipper and Rhonda Shapiro-Rieser

Code 9120
Price: $16.95

Act It Out:

Social Skills for Teens With Autism Spectrum Disorder and Related Disorders

Jeannie Stefonek, M.Ed

Code 9133
Price: $89.95

The Social Times Curriculum

Set includes:
3 Student Books, 1 Teacher Book,1 Curriculum Guide, USB drive with downloadable materials

Kari Dunn Buron

Code 9136B
Price: $89.95

To order, visit www.aapcpublishing.net

6448 Vista Dr.
Shawnee, KS 66218
www.aapcpublishing.net